NAME THAT FEELING

A TURN-AND-SEE BOOK

by Cari Meister

PEBBLE
a capstone imprint

How are you feeling today?
Happy? Mad? Silly? Sad?
You feel lots of different
things all day long.

Read on and guess the feeling
described. Then turn the
page and see if you are right!

Kade was having the best time playing with his friends. But they all had to go home. Now Kade doesn't have anything to do.

How might Kade feel?

turn and see

Bored.

When have you felt bored?

Riley loves to paint, and it's
finally time for art class!

How might Riley feel?

turn and see
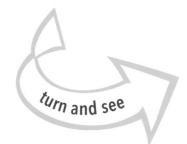

Happy!
When have you felt happy?

Here comes the ball! It zooms right past Eli into the net. The other team wins the game!

How might Eli feel?

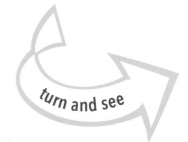
turn and see

Disappointed.

When have you felt disappointed?

Hooray! The carnival is here! Aria and Oliver are going on their first ride.

How might they feel?

turn and see
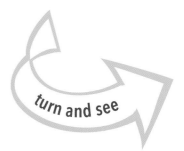

Excited!

When have you felt excited?

Uh-oh! Max stayed up too late reading. His alarm clock beeps and beeps in the morning.

How might Max feel?

turn and see

Grumpy.

When have you felt grumpy?

Imani had a bad day, so her dad
baked her favorite cookies. Yummy!

How might Imani feel?

turn and see

Loved.

When have you felt loved?

Yikes! Look at that mess! Jenny has to clean it up before she can play with her friends.

How might Jenny feel?

turn and see

Mad.

When have you felt mad?

Oh no! Amaya's cat is sick. She has to take her cat to the vet.

How might Amaya feel?

turn and see

Worried.

When have you felt worried?

Reese has a big test coming up. He sits at his desk, focuses, and studies. Then he aces his test!

How might Reese feel?

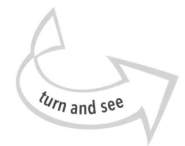
turn and see

Proud!
When have you felt proud?

Bad news! Jade can't go to her friend's house because she is sick.

How might Jade feel?

turn and see

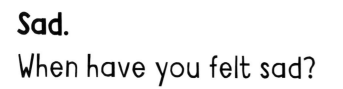

Sad.

When have you felt sad?

Boom! Boom! Thunder rumbles.
Lightning flashes. Micah hides
under his covers.

How might Micah feel?

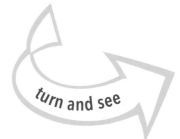

turn and see

Scared.

When have you felt scared?

Ami just moved to a new neighborhood. She doesn't know any of the kids.

How might Ami feel?

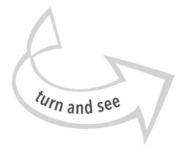

turn and see

Shy.

When have you felt shy?

It's party time! Joe and Ava pick out some props for the photo booth.

How might they feel?

turn and see

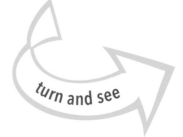

Silly!

When have you felt silly?

Gemma's grandma brought
a new puppy for Gemma.
Gemma couldn't believe it!

How might Gemma feel?

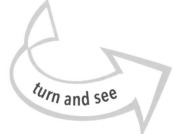
turn and see

Surprised!
When have you felt surprised?

FEELINGS REVIEW

 bored

disappointed

excited

grumpy

happy

loved

mad

 proud

sad

scared

shy

silly

surprised

worried

Pebble Sprout is published by Pebble, an imprint of Capstone.
1710 Roe Crest Drive
North Mankato, Minnesota 56003
www.capstonepub.com

Library of Congress Cataloging-in-Publication Data
Names: Meister, Cari, author.
Title: Name that feeling : a turn-and-see book / by Cari Meister.
Description: North Mankato, MN : Pebble, 2021. | Series: Pebble Sprout: What's
next? | Audience: Ages 6-8 | Audience: Grades 2-3 | Summary: "Lightning flashes.
Thunder rumbles. It's a big storm! How do you think Micah feels? Woof! Woof!
Gemma's grandma brought her a puppy. How do you think Gemma feels?
Turn the page to find out which feeling matches the description. Would you
feel the same way?"— Provided by publisher.
Identifiers: LCCN 2020037980 (print) | LCCN 2020037981 (ebook) |
ISBN 9781977131546 (Hardback) | ISBN 9781977154675 (PDF) | ISBN
9781977156334 (Kindle edition)
Subjects: LCSH: Emotions in children—Juvenile literature. | Expression in
children—Juvenile literature.
Classification: LCC BF723.E6 M47 2021 (print) | LCC BF723.E6 (ebook) | DDC
152.4—dc2
LC record available at https://lccn.loc.gov/2020037980
LC ebook record available at https://lccn.loc.gov/2020037981

Image Credits
Shutterstock: atsurkan, 27, 28, 31; BestPhotoStudio, 21, 22, 31; Blue Planet
Studio, 4, 31; BlurryMe, 30, 31; Brocreative, 10, 31; CCParis, 12, 31; Denis Kuvaev,
6, 31; Dudarev Mikhail, 23; Elena Nichizhenova, 15; Evtushkova Olga, 11; fizkes,
cover, 14, 31; Germanova Antonina, 17; Mark Umbrella, 29; Martin Gardeazabal,
13; matimix, 7; Motortion Films, 5, 24, 31; PR Image Factory, 16, 31; Racheal
Grazias, 9; sirtravelalot, 18, 31; stockfour, 8, 31; Supavadee butradee, 3; Syda
Productions, 19, 20, 31; Teerawat Anothaistaporn, 25, 26, 31

Editorial Credits
Editor: Christianne Jones; Designer: Tracy McCabe; Media Researcher: Morgan
Walters; Production Specialist: Kathy McColley

Printed and bound in the USA. 3837